Day and Night

By Mary Lindeen

Scott Foresman
is an imprint of

Glenview, Illinois • Boston, Massachusetts • Chandler, Arizona •
Upper Saddle River, New Jersey

Photographs

ISBN 13: 978-0-328-46911-6
ISBN 10:   0-328-46911-4

3 4 5 6 7 8 9 10 V010 13 12 11 10

It's the beginning of the day. The first rays of the sun's light are visible in the morning sky.

More sunlight appears in the
morning sky. It's dawn.

The first bit of the sun appears on the eastern horizon. It's the sunrise.

The sun is at its highest point in the daytime sky. The morning is over and the afternoon is beginning. It's noon.

The edge of the sun is slipping down below the western horizon. It's sunset.

The sun has disappeared, but rays of sunlight linger in the western sky. It's dusk.

The sun has set. The sky is dark except for the moon and stars. It's night.

The stars in the dark sky make picture patterns. Look for constellations. There's the Big Dipper and the Little Dipper.

Little Dipper

Big Dipper

It's the middle of the night. It's halfway between evening and morning. It's midnight.

The first rays of the sun's light are visible in the morning sky. It's daybreak once again. Soon it will be dawn. Then the sun will rise on another day.